WHAT IS ZEN?

ALAN WATTS

NEW WORLD LIBRARY
NOVATO, CALIFORNIA

New World Library
14 Pamaron Way
Novato, California 94949

Copyright © 2000 by Mark Watts

Editors: Mark Watts, Marc Allen
Cover design: Mary Ann Casler
Text design: Tona Pearce Myers
Interior calligraphy: Alan Watts

Library of Congress Cataloging-in-Publication Data

Watts, Alan, 1915–1973.
What is zen? / Alan Watts.
p. cm.
ISBN 1-57731-167-1
1. Zen Buddhism—Essence, genius, nature. I. Title.
BQ9265.9.W36 2000
294.3'927—dc21   00-062216

First printing, October 2000
ISBN 1-57731-167-1
Printed in Canada on acid-free, recycled paper
Distributed to the trade by Publishers Group West

10 9 8 7 6 5 4 3 2 1

WHAT IS ZEN?

*"Each one of you
is perfect as you are.
And you all could use
a little bit of improvement."*

— Suzuki Roshi, founder
San Francisco Zen Center

CONTENTS

Introduction by Mark Watts   ix
Preface by Alan Watts   xiii

Part I
A Simple Way, A Difficult Way   19

Part II
Zen Reconsidered   31

Part III
Space   61

Part IV
Zen Mind   95

About the Author   125

Introduction

By Mark Watts

Zen is a method of rediscovering the experience of being alive. It originated in India and China, and has come to the West by way of Japan, and although it is a form of Mahayana Buddhism, it is not a religion in the usual sense of the word. The aim of Zen is to bring about a transformation of consciousness, and to awaken us from the dream world of our endless thoughts so that we experience life as it is in the present moment.

Zen cannot really be taught, but it can be transmitted through sessions of contemplation or meditation, called *zazen*, and through dialogues between student and teacher, called *sanzen*. In the dialogue between the student and Zen master the student comes squarely up against the obstacles to his or her understanding and, without making the answer obvious, the master points a finger toward the way.

Zen has enjoyed an increasing popularity in Western literature. D.T. Suzuki's book *Outlines of Mahayana Buddhism* was first published in the English language in 1907, and authors R. H. Blythe, Christmas Humphries, and Alan Watts all made early contributions to Zen literature in the West. Alan Watts wrote his first booklet on Zen in 1933, followed by his first book, *The Spirit of Zen*, in 1936 at the age of twenty-one. He moved from London to New York in 1938, and after spending nearly ten years in the Anglican Church headed west to California in 1950, where he began to teach Eastern thought at the American Academy of Asian Studies in San Francisco.

There he met Japanese artist Sabro Hasegawa and beat poets Gary Snyder and Allen Ginsburg. His classroom lectures spilled over into the local coffeehouses, and in 1953 he began weekly live radio talks on Pacifica station KPFA in Berkeley, California. Early radio series included "The Great Books of Asia" and "Way Beyond the West," which were later rebroadcast on KPFK in Los Angeles. In 1955 he began work on *The Way of Zen* with the help of a Bollingen grant arranged by Joseph Campbell, and following publication in 1957 he went to New York on the first of many cross-country speaking tours that continued over the next fifteen years.

The selections for *What Is Zen?* were drawn from his later talks, given after he had studied and practiced Zen for many years. Most of the material is from recordings made during weekend seminars in which Watts reconsidered Zen with a small group aboard his waterfront home, the ferryboat SS *Vallejo*, in Sausalito, California.

Instead of focusing on the historical background of Zen, he presented the subject directly, in a way he felt would be most accessible to his primarily Western audience. The result is a unique and effective example of the *sanzen* dialogue in practice, and although the words were delivered to

PREFACE

By Alan Watts

Although not long ago the word *Zen* was unknown to most Europeans and Americans, it has for many centuries been one of the most potent influences in molding the cultures of Japan and China. It would be as great a mistake to leave out the consideration of Zen in a history of Japan as to omit Christianity in a history of England.

Zen remained relatively unknown to the world, however, because until rather recently the exponents of Zen were hesitant to spread the doctrine abroad for fear its essence would be lost. This is because Zen is a practice based entirely upon a certain kind of personal experience, and no complete idea of its truths can be given in words. Finally in the early years of the twentieth century various Far Eastern writers — among them the noted Dr. D.T. Suzuki — made known the details of this remarkable way of life. It then became apparent to Westerners that Zen is responsible for many of the things that fascinate us about the Far East, including the martial arts of *judo* and *aikido* and the exquisite aesthetic flavor that characterizes Chinese and Japanese art.

Many hold Zen to be at one with the root of all religions, for it is a way of liberation that centers around the things that are basic to all mysticism: awakening to the unity or oneness of life, and the inward — as opposed to outward — existence of God. In this context the word God can be misleading because, as will be seen, the idea of a deity in the Western religious sense is foreign to Zen.

The aim of this book is to act as a guide to give the contemporary reader some idea of the basic principles of Zen. My intention is to point out the way by offering the rudiments of the path to those whose search for truth has been hindered by the dogmas, creeds, and misunderstood rituals that choke the road of modern religion.

In the Western world we have become accustomed to thinking of spiritual concerns as being distinct from everyday life. We think of the spiritual as being other worldly, and therefore those art forms that portray spiritual subjects do so with symbols of the divine that transcend everyday materiality.

But in the art of Chinese Zen Buddhism one finds a supreme concentration on the most common aspects of everyday life. Even when the great sages of Buddhism are depicted, they are rendered in a secular style, just like very ordinary people, and more often than not as wandering idiots and tramps. The significance of this extremely human portrayal is that it shows us that their attitude about the relationship of the soul to the body and of mind to matter is entirely different from ours — in fact they do not really consider the spiritual life in those categories at all.

We feel that our soul is separate from the body,

that spirit is separate from matter, and by extension that God is separate from the world. And as we have confronted and tried to reconcile ourselves to this material world we have come to identify ourselves as a kind of detached soul, and therefore we have come to feel that there is a problem with material existence. We believe that life is something that we must conquer, or something we must somehow get out of. But either way we feel distinct from it, and think of ourselves not as a part of the natural material world, but as separate from it, dominating it, and trying to master it.

The art forms of Chinese Buddhism, however, express quite a different point of view, a point of view for which the material, everyday, ordinary world is not a problem to be solved or a conquest to be made.

It would be a bit of relief for us if we could see the world as an extension of ourselves, and ourselves as an extension of the world. In order to understand how Zen came upon this view one must consider the environment in which Zen first arose, which was the native Chinese world of

Taoism. When Buddhism first came to China it was most natural for the Chinese to speak about it in terms of Taoist philosophy, because they both share a view of life as a flowing process in which the mind and consciousness of man is inextricably involved. It is not as if there is a fixed screen of consciousness over which our experience flows and leaves a record. It is that the field of consciousness itself is part of the flowing process, and therefore the mind of man is not a separate entity observing the process from outside, but is integrally involved with it.

As a result, in this philosophy the fundamental conflict between the mind of man and the flow of life is seen to be an illusion, something unreal that we have imagined. This illusion arises because the human memory is a part of this flowing pattern that has the ability to represent former states of the pattern, and this gives the impression of a certain permanence to the behavior of the pattern. We must be aware, however, that our impression of permanence is a kind of thought process that appears to be separate from the pattern upon

PART I

A SIMPLE WAY, A DIFFICULT WAY

A Simple Way,
A Difficult Way

Zen is really extraordinarily simple as long as one doesn't try to be cute about it or beat around the bush! Zen is simply the sensation and the clear understanding that, to put it in Zen terms, there are "ten thousand formations; one suchness." Or you might say, "The ten thousand things that are everything are of one suchness." That is to say that there is behind the multiplicity of events and creatures in this universe simply one energy — and it appears as *you*, and *everything* is it. The practice of Zen is to understand that one energy so as to "feel it in your bones."

Yet Zen has nothing to say about *what* that energy is, and of course this gives the impression in the minds of Westerners that it is a kind of "blind energy." We assume this because the only other alternative that we can imagine in terms of our traditions is that it must be something like God — some sort of cosmic ego, an almost personal intelligent being. But in the Buddhist view, that would be as far off the mark as thinking of it as blind energy. The reason they use the word "suchness" is to leave the whole question open, and absolutely free from definition. It is "such." It is what it is.

The nature of this energy is that it is unformulated, although it is not formless in the sense of some sort of "goo" which is just a featureless mess. It simply means that at the *basis* of everything, there is something that never could be made an *object*, and discerned, figured out, or explained. In the same way, our eyes have no apparent color to us as we look at things, and no form of their own. If they had a form of their own, that form would distort all the forms we see — and in some sense their very structure does distort what we see. If the eyes had a color of their own it would affect everything we see, and still we would never become aware of it. As it is, however, we are not aware of the color of the eye, or of the lens, because if it has a color to it that color is basic to all sight. And so in exactly the same way, you might never become aware of the structure and the nature of the basic energy of the world because *you are it,* and in fact, everything is it.

But you might say, "Well, it really doesn't make any difference then." And that is true, it doesn't — but it *does* make a difference in the life and feeling of a person who realizes that that is so! Although it may not make any particular difference to anything that happens, it points directly to the crux of the matter. If there were no eye, there would be no sight, and this tells us something important about our role in the world. We see this sight and that sight, and the structure of the eye does not make any difference from this sight and that, but upon it depends the possibility of seeing. And so upon this energy depends the very possibility of there being a universe at all, and that is rather important.

It is so important, however, that we usually overlook it. It does not enter into our practical considerations and prognostications, and that is why modern logicians in their respective philosophy departments will argue that all assertions about this energy, including the assertion that it is there at all, are meaningless. And that in a way is true, because the world itself is — from the point of view of strict logic — quite meaningless in the sense that it is not a sign or a symbol pointing to something else. But while that is all taken for granted, it nevertheless makes a great deal of difference to how you *feel* about this world, and therefore, to how you act. If you *know* that there is just this; and that it is you; and that it is beyond time, beyond space, beyond definition; and that if you clearly come to a realization that this is how things are, it gives you a certain "bounce." You can enter into life with abandon, with a freedom from your basic fears that you would not ordinarily have.

You of course can become quite "hooked" on the form of life that you are now living. I can consider myself as "Alan Watts" to be an *immensely* important event — and one I wish to preserve and continue as long as possible! But the truth of the matter is that I know I won't be able to, and that everything falls apart in the end. But if you realize this fundamental energy, then you know you have the prospect of appearing again in innumerable forms, all of which in due course will seem just as important as this one you have now, and perhaps just as problematic too.

This is not something to be believed in, however, because if you believe that this is so upon hearsay, then you have missed the point. You really have no need to believe in this, and you don't need to formulate it, or to hang on to it in any way, because on the one hand you cannot get away from it, and on the other hand you — that is, you in the limited sense — will not be there to experience it. So there is no need to believe in it, and if you do believe in it that simply indicates that you have some doubts in the matter!

That is why Zen has been called the "religion of no religion." You don't need, as it were, to cling to *yourself.* Faith in yourself is not "holding on" to yourself, but letting go. And that is why, when a Zen master hears from a student the statement, "Ten thousand formations, one suchness," the Zen master says, "Get rid of it."

That is also why, in the practice of certain forms of Zen meditation, there is at times a rugged struggle of the person to get beyond *all* formulation whatsoever, and to throw away all hang-ups. Therefore the person endures long hours of sitting with aching knees in perpetual frustration to try to get hold of what all this is about. With tremendous earnestness they say, "I have to find out what the mystery of life is to see who I am and what this energy is."

And so you go again and again to the Zen master, but he knocks down every formulation that you bring to him, because you don't need one. The ordinary person, however, upon hearing that you don't need one, will forget all about it and go on and think about something else, and so they never cross the barrier, and never realize the simplicity and the joy of it all.

But when you do see it, it is totally obvious that there is just one energy, and that consciousness and unconsciousness, being and not-being, life and death are its polarities. It is always undulating in this way: Now you see it, now you don't — now it's here, now it isn't. Because that "on" and "off" *is* the energy, and we wouldn't know what the energy was unless it was vibrating. The only way to vibrate is to go "on" and "off," and so we have life and death, and that's the way it is from our perspective.

That is what Zen is about. And that is all it is about.

Of course, other things derive from that, but in Zen training, the first thing to do is to get the *feeling* of its complete obviousness.

Then what follows from that is the question, "How does a person who feels that way live in this world? What do you do about other people who *don't* see that that's so? What do you do about conducting yourself in this world?"

This is the difficult part of Zen training. There is at first the breakthrough — which involves certain difficulties — but thereafter follows the whole process of learning compassion and tact and skill. As Jesus put it, it is "to be wise as serpents and gentle as doves" — and that is really what takes most of the time.

You might then divide the training in Zen into two stages that correspond to the two great schools of Buddhism: the *Hinayana* stage and the *Mahayana* stage. The Hinayana stage is to get to *nirvana* — to get to "living in the Great Void." But then the Mahayana stage is to "come back," as the Bodhisattva comes back from nirvana out of compassion for all sentient beings to help even the grass to become enlightened. And it's that Mahayana aspect of Zen that occupies most of the time of learning to be proficient in Zen.

I offer this by way of introduction just to make everything clear from the start, and to begin without being deceptive about it or befuddling you with cryptic Zen stories! Although the stories are really quite clear, the point often does not come across very easily to Westerners. The fascinating principle underlying Zen stories with all their seemingly irrelevant remarks is quite simple. It is all explained in the *Sutra of the Sixth Patriarch*, when Hui-neng says,

> *If somebody asks you a question about matters sacred, always answer in terms of matters profane. If they ask you about ultimate reality, answer in terms of everyday life. If they ask you about everyday life, answer in terms of ultimate reality.*

Here's an example: Someone says, "Master, please hand me the knife," and he hands them the knife, blade first. "Please give me the other end," he says. And the master replies, "What would you do with the other end?" This is answering an everyday matter in terms of the metaphysical.

When the question is, "Master, what is the fundamental principle of Buddhism?" then he replies, "There is enough breeze in this fan to keep me cool." That is answering the metaphysical in terms of the everyday, and that is, more or less, the principle Zen works on. The mundane and the sacred are one and the same.

PART II

ZEN
RECONSIDERED

Zen Reconsidered

Why study Zen? The first reason that occurs to me is that it is extremely interesting. Since childhood I have been fascinated by the mystery of being, and it has always struck me as absolutely marvelous that this universe in which we live is here at all. And just out of sheer wonder I have become interested in all of the various answers that people have given as to why all of this is here.

In this sense my approach to religion is not so much that of the moralist as of the scientist. A physicist may have a well-developed and highly concrete experimental approach to nature, but a good physicist is not necessarily an improved man or woman in the sense of being morally superior. Physicists know certain things, and their knowledge is power, but that does not automatically improve them as people. And the power they have may be used for good or for evil.

But indeed, they do have power, and they have gained that power through their knowledge. I have always thought that in many ways Zen is like Western science; Zen has been used for healing people's sicknesses, but it has also been used by the samurai for chopping off people's heads!

I am interested in Zen for what it reveals about the way the universe is, the way nature is, and what this world is doing. My interest is part and parcel of a greater inquiry, which boils down to this: If you read the literature of the great religions, time and time again you come across descriptions of what is usually referred to as "spiritual experience." You will find that in all the various traditions this modality of spiritual experience seems to be the same, whether it occurs in the Christian West, the Islamic Middle East, the Hindu world of Asia, or the Buddhist world. In each culture, it is quite definitely the same experience, and it is characterized by the transcendence of individuality and by a sensation of being one with the total energy of the universe.

This experience has always fascinated me, and I have been interested in the psychological dynamics of it: why it happens, what happens, and how it comes to be described in different symbols with different languages. I wanted to see if I could discover the means of bringing this kind of experience about, because I have often felt that the traditional ways of cultivating it are analogous perhaps to medieval medicine. There a concoction is prepared consisting of roasted toads, rope from the gallows, henbane, mandrake, a boiled red dog, and all manner of such things, and a great brew is made! I assume that someone in the old folk tradition from which these recipes came understood the potencies of the brew, and that this thing really did do some good. But a modern biochemist would take a look at that mixture and say, "Well, it may have done some good, but what was the essential ingredient?"

In the same way, I ask this question when

people sit in Zen meditation, practice yoga, or practice the bhakti way of religious devotion. What is the essential ingredient? In fact I ask this question of all the various things people do, even when they take psychedelic chemicals. No matter what methods people choose, it is interesting to look at what element these methods share in common. If we eliminate the nonsense and the nostalgia that go with people's attachment to a particular cultural approach, what is left?

It has always struck me as a student of these things that Zen has come very close to the essentials. At least this was my first impression, partly because of the way D.T. Suzuki presented Zen. It seemed to me to be the "direct way," the sudden way of seeing right through into one's nature — *right now*, at this moment. There is a good deal of talk about that realization in Zen circles, and in some ways it is more talk than practice. I remember a dinner once with Hasegawa, when somebody asked him, "How long does it take to obtain our understanding of Zen?"

He said, "It may take you three minutes; it may take you thirty years. And," he said, "I mean that."

It is that *three minutes* that tantalizes people! We in the West want instant results, and one of the difficulties of instant results is that they are sometimes of poor quality. I often describe instant coffee as a punishment for people who are in too much of a hurry to make real coffee! There is something to be said against being in a hurry.

There are two sides to this question, and it strikes me in this way: It's not a matter of time at all. The people who think it ought to take a long time are of one school of thought, and the people who want it quickly are of another, and they are both wrong. The transformation of consciousness is not a question of how much time you put into it, as if it were all added up on some sort of quantitative scale, and you got rewarded according to the amount of effort you put into it. Nor is there a way of avoiding the effort just because you happen to be lazy, or because you say, "I want it now!"

The point is, rather, something like this: If you try to get it either by an instant method because you are lazy or by a long-term method because you are rigorous, you'll discover that you can't get it *either* way. The only thing that your effort — or absence of effort — can teach you is that your effort doesn't work.

The answer is found in the middle way — and Buddhism is called the Middle Way — but it is not just some sort of compromise. Instead, "middle" here means instead "above and beyond extremes."

It is put this way in the Bible: "To him that hath shall be given." Or, to put it another way, you can *only* get it when you discover that you don't need it. You can only get it when you *don't* want it. And so instead you ask, "How do I learn *not* to want it, *not* to go after it, either by the long-term method or by the instant method?" But obviously if you ask that, you still are seeking it, and thereby not getting it!

A Zen master says, "If you have a stick, I will give you one. If you have not, I will take it away from you." Of course this is the same idea as "to him that hath shall be given; and from him that hath not, shall be taken away even that which he hath." So we find ourselves in a situation where it seems that all our normal thinking — all the ways we are accustomed to thinking about solving problems — doesn't work. All thinking based on acquisition is rendered obsolete. We have, as it were, to get into a new dimension altogether to approach this question.

A young Zen student I know said to me recently, "If I were asked what is really essential in Zen, it would be *sanzen*." Sanzen is the dialogue between the master and the student, the person-to-person contact. He said rather than *zazen*, or sitting meditation, it is *sanzen* that is the crux of it. It is in the peculiar circumstances of that dialog that we can get into the frame of mind I am talking about.

In effect this dialog acts as a mirror to one's own mind, because the teacher always throws back to the student the question he's asked! He really does not answer any questions at all, he merely tosses them back at you, so that you yourself will ask *why* you are asking it, and why you are creating the problem the question expresses.

And quickly it becomes apparent that it is up to you. "Who, *me?*" you may ask. *Yes, you!* "Well," you may say, "I can't solve this problem. I don't know how to do it."

But what do you mean by *you?* Who are you, really? Show me the you that cannot answer the question. It is in this kind of back-and-forth dialogue that you begin to understand. Through relationship with the other person you discover that it is you who's mixed up, and that you are asking the wrong questions! In fact, you are trying to solve the wrong problem altogether.

There is a curious thing about gurus — including Zen masters: you notice how people feel that gurus have marvelous eyes, and that they look right through you. And people think, "Oh dear me, they can see to the bottom of my soul. They can read my history, my secret thoughts, my awful misdeeds, and everything. At one glance they know me through and through!"

Such matters are of very little interest to real gurus, however. When they look at you with a funny look, they see who you *really* are, and are looking through your eyes to the divine center.

And here one sees Buddha, Brahma, or whatever you want to call it, pretending not to be at home! It's no wonder the guru has a funny look — they are beholding the incongruity between the divine being that looks out through you in your eyes, and the expression of puzzlement on your face! And so what the guru is going to do in the dialog is to "kid" you out of this irresponsibility — this playing that you are someone other than who you really are. And this, you see, is of the essence.

Don't mistake me, however: I am not saying in order to get there you have to have a guru, and have to go and find one somewhere. That, too, is to go back into the ordinary dimension, back into a state of inner irresponsibility. It is important to realize that *you* give the gurus their authority to do what they do. It is you who says, "be my teacher" — and in Zen they make it very tough for you to get a teacher at all. The Hindus do likewise, and they have various ways of explaining that gurus have to take on the karma of their students, and that is a dangerous thing to do because they become responsible for their students. But this is

So if you accept that, and say, "I'll go study Zen here," do you see what is happening? You have made the decision to use this group as a pretext upon which to project your own authority without realizing that *you* have done it!

You set the whole thing up, and then the task of the teacher is to show you just what you did. But it all came from you. As the Buddhists say, "All this world is in your own mind."

In the *Tibetan Book of the Dead*, when the instructions are given as to what happens when someone leaves their body after death, it says something like, "When the clear light of the void comes, it is followed by the vision of the blissful Bodhisattvas; then comes the vision of the wrathful Bodhisattvas," and so on. And then it says, "Realize, oh nobly born, that all this is but the outpouring of your own mind."

We don't accept this very easily, however, because we've been most assiduously taught that we are but "little things" in this world. You must be humble, after all, you did not create this world, somebody *else* made it. So watch your "p's" and "q's," and do not for one minute have the spiritual pride of thinking that you are the cause of it all!

And you may very well ask, "How could I have made all this? I certainly don't know how it was made!" But a Zen poem says,

> *If you want to ask where the flowers come from,*
> *even the God of Spring doesn't know.*

There is no way of defining the creative energy of the universe. Suppose God could come and talk to you, and you said, "God, this is a pretty complicated universe — in fact, it is amazing! How did you do it?" And God would say, "I don't know, I just did it."

Of course God does not know — if God had to think out every detail of it, it never would have happened. In just the same way, you breathe and you live: You don't know how you do it, but you are still doing it!

We have been taught by social convention, though, to restrict the concept of "myself" to "what I do voluntarily and consciously." This is a very narrow view of the self. Certainly if you say, "I, by my ego and my intelligence, created all this," you would be conceited, and you know you are a liar. But *you* is much deeper than that; *you* includes far more than your conscious mind. It is the *total you* that not only is responsible for the infinitely complex structure of your physical organism, but also for the environment in which you find yourself. *You* runs that deep.

It is you in that sense, the *total you*, that is the root and ground of everything. And yet we arrange our image of who we are around a principle of human sociability, which is measured by our ability to get along together according to our system of social convention. And as a result we so often end up putting everyone down, including ourselves, because nobody's perfect, and because, as my mother used to say to me, "You're not the only pebble on the beach!"

Why don't we instead try the other technique, and put everyone "up" instead of down? It might be that everyone would get along far better that way than they do by putting everybody down! Of course, whatever you do, you have to do it uniformly for everyone. You can't say, "Well, Johnny is the Lord God, but Peter isn't!"

As a result of our social conventions, we all feel ourselves to be strangers in the world. We are disconnected from it all, and it is something that "happens" to us that we endure passively, and that we *receive* passively. And we never get to the point where we realize we are actually doing the whole thing! It is up to *you.* You make your troubles, and you put yourself into a trap. You confuse yourself, and forget that you did it, and then ask how to get out of it! A verse from the *Mumonkan*, a famous book of *koans*, puts it this way: "Asking where Buddha is, is like hiding loot in your pocket and declaring yourself innocent!"

To finally admit it, and to come to the recognition that it was you, requires a certain kind of nerve. I don't mean "nerve" in the sense of being brash and cheeky. I mean the sort of sense that you use when, for the first time, you take a plane off the ground, or when you pull a cloth off the table and leave all the dishes on the table! *That* sort of nerve has nothing to do with pride in the ordinary sense. It is being ready to leap in, somehow. You see it, and jump in.

But most of us lack that kind of sense. Instead we have what I would call an ambivalent sense of responsibility. We say, "Now, look: It is only me here — just little me. I have certain responsibilities, and they are such and so, but that means as well that there are a lot of things I am certainly not responsible for." And in our social conventions we play games about where we are going to draw the line that defines what we are — and what we're not — responsible for.

When someone is in some kind of social or psychological difficulty, and someone has been irresponsible in some way, we wonder what caused the problem: "*Why* are they like that?" And instead of attributing the problem to the person, our psychologists tend to refer it back to other things and other people: It was because of their environment, or because of family conditioning, or because of their father and mother. But there is no end to that, because you can take the blame straight back to

Adam and Eve! And responsibility is evaded, because it was limited in the first place.

We think that the world is limited and explained by its past. We tend to think that what happened in the past determines what is going to happen next, and we do not see that it is exactly the other way around! What is always the source of the world is the *present*; the past doesn't explain a thing. The past trails behind the present like the wake of a ship, and eventually disappears.

Now you would say that obviously when you see a ship crossing the ocean with the wake trailing behind it that the *ship* is the cause of the wake. But if you get into the state of mind that believes in causality as we do, you see that the *wake* is the cause of the ship! And that is surely making the tail wag the dog!

The point is this: You will never find the mystery of the creation of the world in the past. It never was created in the past. Because truly there *is* nothing else — and never was anything else — except the present! There never will be anything else except the present.

Life is always present, and the past is a kind of echo, a tracing within the present of what the present did before. We can say, "Oh well, we can guess what the present will do next because of what it has done in the past." And this is true: Because of what it does habitually, you may guess it will go on doing it like that. But still it is not the past that controls the present any more than the wake controls the ship. Now from the record of the past you can study the nature of the present and predict what sort of things it's likely to do. But sometimes it surprises you when something new happens, as every so often it does.

It is always in the immediate here and now that things begin. And so, one of the essentials of Zen training is, to quote a certain parrot from Huxley's *Island*, "Here and now, boys!" *Be here.*

And in order to be here, you can't be looking for a result! People keep asking me, "Why do you do this? What do you want to get out of it?" But these questions imply that my motivation is different from my action. It is talking about it in terms of Newtonian billiards — in Newton's explanation of mechanics and behavior he used an analogy with billiards. The balls — the fundamental atoms — are banging each other about; a ball will be still until something bangs it, and that bang will be its motivation, and set it in motion. So when we say, "Human beings behave in such-and-such a way because of unconscious mental mechanisms," this is really Newtonian psychology, and it is out-of-date. Today we need a psychology that is current with quantum theory at least, not one that is tied to mechanical causality.

It is difficult for us to understand this, however, unless we turn things around, as in the analogy of the ship and the wake. If you understand fully that it is from the present that everything happens, then the only place for you to be, the only place for you to live, is here, right now.

People immediately say, however, "Now wait a minute. That's all very well, but I want to be sure that under such-and-such circumstances and in such-and-such eventualities I will be able to deal with it. It's all very well to live in the present when I am sitting comfortably in a warm room reading this, or meditating, but what am I going to do if all hell breaks loose? What if there's an earthquake, or if I get sick, or my best friends get sick, or some catastrophe happens? How will I deal with that? Don't I have to prepare myself to deal with those things? Shouldn't I get into some sort of psychological training, so that when disasters come I won't be thrown?"

That, you would ordinarily think, is the way to proceed — but it doesn't work very well. It is much better to say, "sufficient unto the day is the trouble thereof," and to trust yourself to react appropriately when the catastrophe happens. Whatever happens, you'll probably have to improvise, and failure of nerve is really failure to trust yourself. You have a great endowment of brain, muscle, sensitivity, intelligence — trust it to react to circumstances as they arise.

Zen deals with this. Studying Zen will change the way you react to circumstances as they arise. Wait and see how you deal with whatever circumstances come your way, because the you that will deal with them will not be simply your conscious intelligence or conscious attention. In that moment it will be *all* of you, and that is beyond the control of the will, because the will is only a fragment having certain limited functions.

But if you really know how to live from your center, you live *now*, and know that *now* is the origin of everything. This way, you stand a much better chance of being able to deal with the unforeseen than if you keep worrying about it and considering past lessons and future possibilities.

I know that this sounds impractical to some of you, or perhaps revolutionary, or perhaps not even possible, but it is simply living in the present. It requires a certain kind of poise: If you make exact plans to deal with the future and things don't happen at all as you expected, you are apt to become thoroughly disappointed and disoriented. But if your plans are flexible and adaptable, and if you're *here* when things happen, you always stay balanced.

As in movement or martial arts, keep your center of gravity between your feet, and don't cross your feet, because the moment you do you are off balance. Stay always in the center position, and stay always *here.* Then it doesn't matter which direction the attack comes from; it doesn't matter what happens at all.

If you expect something to come in a certain way, you position yourself to get ready for it. If it comes another way, by the time you reposition your energy, it is too late. So stay in the center, and you will be ready to move in any direction.

This is the real meaning of the practice of *zazen,* or sitting Zen: to sit in the center. As you begin sitting meditation the first thing to do is to find your center, and become comfortable with it, so that you are neither leaning forward nor sitting back. When one's body is balanced in this way the forces of high and low, the heart and breath, and mind and feeling merge at the center.

To sit in zazen in order to perfect a technique for attaining enlightenment, however, is fundamentally a mistaken approach. Sit just to sit. And why not sit? You have to sit sometime, and so you may as well *really* sit, and be altogether here. Otherwise the mind wanders away from the matter at hand,

and away from the present. Even to think through the implications of the present is to avoid the present moment completely.

When you are meditating, it is perfectly fine to be aware of anything that's around: things on the floor, the smell of the atmosphere, the little noises going on. Be there! But when you hear a dog bark, and that starts off a train of thought about dogs in general, about your dog, or somebody else's dog, then you have wandered away from being *here.* Of course you finally will come to the point where you realize there is no way of wandering away from being here, because there is nowhere else to be. Even if you think about somewhere else, past or future, this is all happening *now.*

Through this you will also come to understand how to be a scholar and a historian, if you wish to, and still live in the present. That was how D.T. Suzuki was able to be scholarly and intellectual, and yet at the same time not to depart at all from the spirit of Zen, which is beyond the intellect. You can intellectualize in a Zen way, just as you can sweep floors in a Zen way, but of course the key to the matter is centering — *being really here.* Because this is the point of origin of the world, and it is at the same time the destination of the world.

This is the real meaning of *dhyana*, which in Sanskrit is the kind of concentration or meditation that constitutes Zen. Zen is simply the Japanese way of pronouncing dhyana, and it is that state of centeredness which is here and now.

When you practice zazen, just sit and enjoy yourself being quiet. It is not a duty at all; it is a great pleasure! Get up early in the morning when the sunlight is just beginning to show. It doesn't matter where you are, just sit.

Don't have any thoughts, but don't compulsively try to get rid of thoughts. It's just not important. The real thing is *what is* — what is here, now. After all, here you are, and you may as well see it!

Eventually, a curious feeling will overcome you, one that is very hard to describe in words. I just said that the origin of the world is now — and there is this odd sensation that now comprises everything: the most distant past, the most remote future, the vastness of space, all states of experience, all joy, all sorrow, all heights, all depths. Everything is now. There isn't anywhere else to be — there never was, and never will be!

That is why you never were born, and therefore cannot die. You never came, so you won't go. You were always here. It's a very curious feeling, so different from what we ordinarily think. In entering into the now, we find the *eternal now*. We find infinity in the split second.

As they say in Yoga, liberation lies in the interval between two thoughts. Between the past thought and the future thought lies *now* — there is no present thought.

As one of the Zen texts puts it, "One thought follows another without interruption. But if you allow these thoughts to link up into a chain, you put yourself in bondage."

Actually, this present moment never comes to be and it never ceases to be, it is simply our minds that construct the continuity of thoughts we call time. In the present moment is *nirvana*.

As the great Zen master Dogen explains, in the

course of the seasons, the spring does not "become" the summer. And when wood burns, the wood does not "become" the ashes. There is the state of wood, and then there is the state of ashes. There is the state of spring; there is the state of summer. The spring does not become the summer; the wood does not become ashes; the living body does not become the corpse. That only happens in us, in our minds, when we link our thoughts together. "Oh, no! I will become a corpse!" But you won't. You won't be there when there is a corpse!

If we are going to introduce Westerners to the fundamentals of Zen, we need to revise our understanding of the procedures and rationale of meditation. It should not become a competitive game of one-upmanship, or a marathon to see who can take it, and who can endure. That puts the whole affair right back under the domain of time.

The important thing to emphasize is *presence*, being completely here, and not feeling guilty if you enjoy it. You can do that most easily in any kind of activity that does not require much discursive thought. Anything that you can do without a great deal of thought becomes a perfect form of meditation, whether it's shucking peas, digging up a plot of ground, putting up a fence, or doing dishes.

In Buddhism one hears of "the four dignities of man." It is an extraordinary phrase, when you think about it, especially when you learn the "four dignities" are simply walking, standing, sitting, and lying. Zazen is simply "sitting Zen." There is also "lying Zen," which is sleeping Zen — when you sleep, sleep. There is "standing Zen," and there is "walking Zen." Walking is a very good method of meditation. You simply stroll around, but be right with it! Be *here*.

People have difficulties with these simple forms of meditation. Thoughts and feelings come up: "Is it only this? Is this all there is? Nothing seems to be happening. What's going on? I feel a little frustrated, and I don't particularly feel enlightened. There's just nothing 'special' about this at all. Do I have to do this longer in order for something to happen?"

But nothing special is supposed to happen. It's just *this*. This is it, right here.

You may have difficulty in accepting it because you still feel the lack of nerve to see that *you are all of it*. You are not an observer who is witnessing the present moment as something happening to you. The present that you are experiencing is all of you. It's not "you" here looking at "the floor" there. The floor is just as much you as the organism looking at it. You are doing the floor, just like you're doing your feet. It is all one world — and you're responsible for it.

So enjoy it! Have a good time!

PART III

SPACE

SPACE

Zen represents a simplified way of life. The style and way in which a Zen temple is furnished is completely uncluttered. The rooms of a temple are mostly empty. They are just spaces — but they are *gorgeous* spaces.

Space is the most valuable thing in Japan, and it is treated with great reverence. Here in the United States, where we have so much space, we do not appreciate it. We think that space is equivalent to "nothing," something that simply isn't there. We think of space as a "blank," but in a more crowded situation, people really notice space.

It is interesting that China too is a country

where there is also a lot of space, yet I think it was the Chinese who above all through the arts first taught man to appreciate space. Today we are living in a "space age" and, strangely enough, even though our culture is a pioneer in space navigation and space exploration, we really don't understand the value of space at all. One of the great contributions of Zen to the Western world is understanding space.

The most desirable land for residences in Japan is in the hills. The hills are full of parks and water springs, but the curious thing is that the best land and the most gorgeous sites are occupied by Zen temples. These temples were originally taken away from the brigands, who somehow let the Zen monks come in. These monks essentially put one over on the brigands and occupied the space.

In the Kamakura epoch, Zen had an enormous influence on the samurai warrior caste. This was a time when Japan was torn by internal strife, and constant war was waged between the various feudal lords as they fought to gain control of the imperial power. They went to study Zen as soldiers in order to learn fearlessness — and that was where the Zen monks outfoxed the samurai. The samurai prided themselves on their manly and warrior-like qualities, but they couldn't scare the Zen monks because the monks were just not fazed — not stopped at all — by the idea of death!

A classic Zen story about their fearlessness is the tale of a young man who applied to a fencing master to be his student. The master looked at him and said, "Who did you study with before?"

He said, "I've never studied fencing before."

The master looked at him in a funny way and said, "No, surely, come now, you have studied with someone."

He said, "No sir, I never have studied."

"Well," the master said, "I'm an experienced teacher, and I can tell at once by looking at a person whether he has studied fencing or not. And I know you have!"

But the young man shook his head and said, "Sir, I assure you, I've never studied fencing at all with anybody."

"Well," said the master, "there must be something peculiar about you — what do you suppose it could be?"

"Well," the young man said, "when I was a boy, I was very worried about dying. So I thought a great deal about death. And then I came to the realization that there's nothing in death to be afraid of."

"Oh," said the master, "that explains it."

One of the results of the initial part of Zen training — the beginning of Zen — is overcoming the fear of death. What I described to you earlier as the Hinayana stage of Zen study is where you go deeply into meditation and withdraw your consciousness, as it were, back to its source.

This is the initial stage, and as you go into it, you go down into that dimension of your being where you are deeper than your individuality. And you realize that you belong down here, because this is where you truly exist. What you *feel* as your individuality is really something temporal, like the leaves of a deciduous tree. In the season of the fall, they dry up and drop off.

The Japanese in their poetry and aesthetics always liken death to the fall and winter season. They have a feeling about a human life that is harmonious with the seasons of the year. This theme goes through Japanese poetry, and therefore old people are looked upon as those who are in the "winter" of life, or the "fall" of life. And just as the maple trees in Japan become absolutely gorgeous in the fall, there is an appreciation and a respect for this season of life. Old people in Japan look much better than our old people because they're not fighting with age, they're cooperating with it. It is an honorable thing to be old.

For women and for men, age means respect and authority. This feeling of the harmoniousness of human life with the life cycles of nature makes aging and death less problematic for people with that sort of psychology. They see old age as the proper rhythm of time, not as the deterioration of a living being, just as they don't see the fall and winter as a deterioration of time.

I suppose this may be a difficult correspondence for us to understand, because we simply don't feel the seasons in the same way. So many of us live in a seasonless world.

I mentioned earlier the idea that the great Zen master Dogen put in his book, the *Shobogenzo* — actually, he got the idea from a Chinese student of Kumarajiva, who lived about A.D. 400. Dogen noted that, contrary to appearance, events in time are eternal, and that each event "stays" in its own place. The burning wood does not become ash. First there is wood and then there is ash. The spring does not become the summer. There is spring, then there is summer; then there is fall, then there is winter.

And, curious as it may sound, the sun in its rotation does not move, and the river doesn't flood. It sounds paradoxical to us. It's like the saying from Heraclitus: You never step into the same river twice.

There is a very close parallel between the thinking of Heraclitus and Taoist philosophy; both understand the yang and the yin. Heraclitus is the most original thinker in Western thought. (Phillip Wheelwright published an excellent translation of what remains of the fragments of Heraclitus' philosophy.) If the West had founded itself on Heroclitus rather than Aristotle, we would have been a lot better off, because he was a most ingenious man, and his thought is far closer to Eastern thought.

The Japanese feel that death is a completely natural event; it is only, as it were, the dropping of the leaves, and yet the root underneath is always there. This is difficult for most people to appreciate; the root doesn't seem to enter into our ordinary lives at all. "I feel that I'm only 'on top' — how do I 'get down'?" Well of course the *top* is the top and it can't get down and be the *bottom!*

This is the same question people raise when they ask, "How do I get rid of my egocentricity?" Well, obviously, you can't get rid of egocentricity with your egocentricity — as the master Bankei said, "You can't wash off blood with blood!" And *trying* to realize your Buddha-nature by some sort of egocentric effort is like trying to wash off your ego with your ego, and blood with blood.

In his teaching Bankei emphasized the way in which you have this root in you. He said, "When you hear a bell ringing, you don't have to think about it — you know at once that it's a bell. When you hear the crow cawing, you don't by any effort or cleverness of your conscious will know that it's a crow — your mind does that for you."

Once Bankei was being heckled by a Nichiren priest — those Nichirens can be very fanatical. The Nichiren priest was standing on the fringe of a crowd listening to Bankei, and he called out, "I don't understand a single word you're saying!"

And Bankei said, "Come closer, and I'll explain it to you."

So the priest walked into the crowd, and Bankei said, "Come on, come closer."

And he came closer. "Come closer still!" And he came closer. "Please, closer still" — until he was right next to Bankei. And Bankei said, "How well you understand me!"

Bankei emphasized that we have what he called the "unborn mind" in us, the level of mind that doesn't arise, that isn't born into individuality. We all have that original endowment. When somebody says "good morning," we say "good morning," and we don't "think" to do this — that's the unborn mind. It's the unborn mind through which your eyes are blue or brown; it's the unborn mind by which you see and breathe.

Breathing is important in the practice of meditation because it is the faculty in us that is simultaneously voluntary and involuntary. You can feel that you are breathing, and equally you can feel that it is breathing you. So it is a sort of bridge between the voluntary world and the involuntary world — a place where they are one.

Through focusing on our breathing, and by understanding this concept, we can acquire the sense that our unconscious life is not unconscious at all, in the sense that it lacks consciousness; instead, it is the root of consciousness, the source from which consciousness comes. Just as the leaves come every year on the tree, so consciousness perpetually comes and goes out of the unconscious base, or what we could call the *supra*-conscious base.

In order to appreciate this, you don't need to believe literally in reincarnation — the idea that you have an individual, enduring center or soul that is born into existence time after time after time. Zen practitioners are divided as to whether they think this is so or not. I've met masters who believe in reincarnation, and I've met masters who don't believe in it at all.

When they talk of the continual reappearance of individuality and consciousness out of the base, what they mean is simply something all of us can see: We see human beings in all stages of life coming and going. We don't see any continuity between them.

But that is only because we don't see *space*. It is the interval between people — the space between lives — that constitutes the bond between them. This is very important — the philosophy of space — and we will get into it in more depth, but the point here is that through realizing this, those Zen monks had enormous nerve. They could look a samurai in the face and say, "Okay, cut my head off! What does it prove?"

The samurai were amazed by this, and regarded those monks as sort of magical people. They asked the monks to teach them, because they felt if they had that kind of fearlessness, they could never be defeated by an enemy.

Zen is like a spring coming out of a mountain. It doesn't flow out in order to quench the thirst of a traveler, but if the travelers want to help themselves to it, that's fine. It's up to you what you do with the water; the spring's job is just to flow. Zen masters will teach anyone who has the tenacity to go after it, whoever they are. The samurai became grateful students of the Zen monks, and let them occupy the best land in town!

On that land they built buildings that are essentially great, heavy roofs in the Tang Dynasty Chinese style supported by a kind of elegant flimsiness underneath. They're like lanterns — under the roof, empty floors are covered with straw mats; there are sliding screens, and occasional cushions to sit on, and *nothing* else. You get a feeling of "living" space inside.

Let's consider that a moment. I said earlier that in the West we disregard space. We know space here on the planet is full of air, and we know that is "something." Air occupies space and is very important to us, essential to life in fact, but we think of air as simply filling a "void." When astronomers start to talk about curved space, or properties of space, the average person feels that their common sense has been offended. "How could space be curved? How could it have any properties? It isn't there. It's nothing!"

But the folly of thinking that way becomes apparent the moment you realize that solidness, materiality, or density is inconceivable apart from space. Space is the interval between solids, and thus in some sense is the relationship between them.

To understand this, consider for a moment another kind of space altogether: "musical" space

— the interval between notes in a melody. When you play a sequence of notes in a melody, there is no pause, no silence between one note and another; they follow each other immediately. But it is only because of the interval — something that is not stated, *not* "sounded" — that you hear a melody. If you don't hear the interval, you don't hear the melody. The space between the notes, the step, the interval is an essential element in melody. In exactly the same way, it is space — be it interior space or interstellar space — that goes hand in hand with there being any solids or stars. Space isn't just "nothing," it is the other pole of something.

Let's look at it from another point of view. We have looked at space astronomically, and musically; let's look at it for a moment aesthetically. In a motel room, for example, when you see the typical "Western" flower print — for some reason or other hotels and motels love flower or bird prints in frames over the bed — you see a bunch of flowers set directly in the middle of a piece of paper. This shows that the person who designed the print has no conception of space, because the space in that print serves merely as background, and is nothing more. It has no function whatsoever; the space is not part of the picture.

When Chinese painters use space, however, you see that if they paint a spray of grass or bamboo or a pine tree, they never set it directly in the middle of the paper. It is set off to one side, so that the object painted is, as we say, "balanced" by the space, and the space is an essential part of the painting. By putting the spray of bamboo to one side, you immediately see the part of the painting that hasn't been touched as *something* — as mist, or even water. The painter doesn't have to do a thing to it — somehow it is all in the picture. The bamboo is not merely set against the background — everything right out to the edge of the piece of paper has been included in the piece by doing this. The artist sees the polarity of space and solid, and uses this polarity in the painting by balancing them against each other.

But you do not feel that balance if the solid area — the painted subject, whatever it may be — is put smack in the middle of the space. Instead, you abolish the importance of the space; it has no "place" in the painting. When we think of a solid object simply sitting in the middle of a canvas, we ignore space.

I have had great fun when visiting college communities by doing experiments in Gestalt psychology that illustrate figure and ground. The Gestalt theory of perception is that we tend to notice the figure and ignore the background. We tend to notice a moving object and ignore what is relatively still. We tend to notice areas that are tightly enclosed rather than those that are diffused.

I draw a circle on the blackboard and say to the group, "What have I drawn?" They inevitably say, "A circle, a ball, a ring," or something like that. And I say then, "Why didn't anybody suggest that I have drawn a wall with a *hole* in it?" It shows us that we tend to ignore the background and pay attention to the figure.

Western artists almost inevitably paint the entire background, because they don't realize that "empty" space is important.

Architects, however, will talk about the "properties" of a space, because they know that what they're doing is making *living* spaces for people. They are enclosing space, and so space has a certain reality to the architect. But to the ordinary person, space just isn't there! We're not aware of it.

It's very interesting that in meditation experiments you can experience various kinds of space: optical space, auditory space, and tactile space. By closing your eyes for a while, you can realize what a blind man's conception of space would be. Every sense has its own appreciation of space.

There was a time in our own history when we can see, by reading between the lines of ancient literature — as late as Dante — that they regarded "space" and "mind" as the same thing. And if you think about it, you can see it is rather obvious. Take the "mind of the eye" — what Buddhists call the *vijnana* — which corresponds to seeing. The basis of sight is a sort of screen, and just as you have a screen on which to project a slide or a movie, there is a kind of ground or area in which everything that is seen must be. You have what we call a "field of vision," which is an oval, with fuzzy edges. You "see" an oval area, this field of vision. There has to be that open field for there to be any vision at all and, though we ignore it, it is the background.

There was once an Englishman and an Indian sitting in a garden together, and the Hindu was trying to explain basic Indian philosophy to the Englishman. So he said, "Look now, there is a hedge at the end of the garden — against what do you see the hedge?"

The Englishman said, "Against the hills."

"And what do you see the hills against?"

He said, "Against the sky."

"And what do you see the sky against?" And the Englishman didn't know what to say.

So the Hindu said, "You see it against conscious-ness."

In the same way, the space for "being" itself — for material vibration — is the space that we think of as existing between bodies. That is the ground

— the field — which quanta must have in order to play. In the same way that space itself is invisible, consciousness is unknown, because it is not an object of our knowledge. This dimension of your being is like space. This basis is called *amala vijnana* in Buddhist teachings, and it means "without taint." You can't make a mark on space!

The Buddha said, "The path of the enlightened ones leaves no track — it is like the path of birds in the sky."

The Buddhists describe the ultimate reality of the world as *shunyata*, which is often translated as "emptiness" or "the void," or even "the plenum void," meaning it is void, but full of all possibilities. The basic doctrine of Buddhist Mahayana philosophy is given in the *Heart Sutra*:

Form is emptiness; emptiness is form.

To indicate this idea in Chinese, they use a character for *shunyata* or emptiness that also means "sky" and "space." Space is contrasted with the word for form (which also means "shape" and "color"), and the character between them means something like "exactly is" — *space exactly is, or is precisely the same as form*. And when the characters are reversed it says form is precisely emptiness.

The Chinese word for "is," however, is not quite the same as the English or European "is" (in Latin *est)*; it means rather "is inseparable from," or "always goes with." The two are interdependent. You can't have space without form; you can't have form without space. They are relational, and in that sense, they *are* each other, because underneath every inseparable relation is a common ground.

To perceive that form reveals the void, and to see that the void reveals form, is the secret for the overcoming of death. To the extent that one is unaware of space, one is unaware of one's own eternity — it's the same thing!

People sometimes imagine that to be aware of the eternal dimension, the forms must disappear. This belief is held by many in India who believe that in *nirvikalpa samadhi*, which is the highest state of consciousness (*samadhi* means the meditation state; concentration; absorption into ultimate reality beyond words; *nirvikalpa* means without concept), is without "content." They will say that in the state of *nirvikalpa* the mind is completely devoid of *any form or motion* whatsoever.

That sounds like a total "blank." And in Zen it is said that a person whose mind is in that state is a "stone" Buddha, just like the Buddha made of stone sitting on the altar: there is no consciousness. There's no point in that, and so in Zen they interpret all this in a very different way indeed. To have *nirvikalpa samadhi*, the highest state of consciousness, is not to have consciousness in which there are no forms, it is simply to reawaken to the *reality* of space. To see that forms come and go in space as the leaves come and go on the trees, as the stars come and go in the sky.

The sky is in a way the mother of the stars, and of course no woman is a mother until she has a child. So in this sense space does not come into being as the matrix of the world until there is something there to nurture. That's why the Chinese use the term "to arise mutually" to indicate the relationship between all opposites: they come into being, they arise mutually.

Space and form arise mutually — as do being and non-being. Then you can see what it means in practical life: To the degree that you are unaware of space, you are unaware of the fullness of your nature.

As our population increases, and we become more crowded, space will become more valuable, and this will help us to be more aware of it. Perhaps that's the reason why species multiply: as *many-ness* increases, the consciousness of *one-ness* increases.

So in Zen, in answer to the question, "What is the ultimate reality?" the master says, "Three pounds of flax."

He chooses something very particular, extremely concrete and "everyday" — something quite worldly — to answer this metaphysical question. Why? Because space does not obliterate the particular, but rather it is precisely the particular, ordinary everyday event that proclaims and advertises the underlying unity of the world.

The many advertise the one — the solid implies and indeed exhibits and brings out the fact that there is space. Were there no solids, there would be no space. If you try to imagine space with no solids, you have to get rid of *yourself* looking at it, because you're a solid in the middle of the space! Space, space, space forever — with nothing in it — is absolutely meaningless, an unimaginable concept. You have to have space and solid — they always go together.

This explains some of the many ways in which Zen life has feeling for space. Here's another very different thing to consider: their idea of poverty. The poverty of the monk, for example, is not poverty as we have thought of it in the Western tradition. It is not poverty as a sort of oppression, where the poor are deprived and feel denuded by poverty. In Zen, poverty is voluntary, and considered not really as poverty so much as simplicity, freedom, unclutteredness.

They have the same feeling for it as they do for purity. The "pure" mind — the "taintless" mind —

means not that you are a "prude," in any sense, because they don't think of purity in that sense at all. It does not mean not having any appetites — not feeling hungry, never feeling sexual, or anything like that! In Zen, purity means "clarity." A "pure" eye is a clear eye — without dust in it, just as a pure mirror is a mirror without dust. But the real prototype of purity in Buddhist literature is not so much the mirror as *space* itself. That is purity, clarity, transparency; it is also freedom.

Purity and poverty are simply an absence of pain.

The peculiarly noticeable thing about the personality of Zen people is the uncluttered mind. When you deal with Zen masters, you have a strange feeling that so long as you are with them and addressing them, they are absolutely *with* you. They have nothing else to do but to talk to you. They are just "right there."

They're willing to have some "small talk." They're not like those terribly serious spiritual people who have no time for small talk at all and who can't just pass the time of day! But on the other hand they don't waste time. They don't dither around, and they're never distracted. When something is finished, it's *finished*; and they go right on to the next thing.

You can see this in the way they walk. They have a characteristic walk that is quite different from other Japanese people's walk. This may be partly due to dress, because Zen monks have a wide skirt on their robes, and they stride as they walk, with a kind of a rhythm that is completely characteristic. A Zen monk walking down the street is exactly like a cat crossing the road. When you see a cat crossing the road, the cat always looks as if it knows exactly where it's going. Both cats and Zen monks move in a way that conveys a feeling of freedom.

I stayed one time in an inn on the edge of Nanzengi in the northern corner of Kyoto. I got up early, as I usually do, and sat on the balcony. In the distance I heard this sound: "*Hoa! Hoa! Hoa!*" It came nearer and nearer; then I saw these monks with their big mushroom hats on and their begging bowls held out in front of them. *Hoa* means "the dharma."

They came down the street with a swinging, rhythmic walk: boom-boom-boom-boom-boom! I thought I'd put something in their bowls, and I shot downstairs. But by the time I got there, they were gone.

We had dinner in the monastery that night and I told the priest who was entertaining us about this incident, and said, "You know, I don't think your monks are *serious* about begging! In the early morning the little cart comes with groceries, and it stays around long enough for the housewives to come out and buy their vegetables. At night, there comes a man who sells ramen (noodle soup) on a little cart, and he stays around long enough for people to come out. But your monks don't stay around long enough for anybody to give them anything! I don't think they're really begging at all; they're just fat and rich and their begging is a gesture!"

The next morning I went down early, and stood on the lower level. The monks came by, but they weren't begging at all. They carried their big mushroom hats in their hands in front of them, pointing outwards — the way they hold them when they're just walking, and not begging. There were about three of them walking single-file, Indian style, and the lead monk looked at me and bowed with a kind of evil grin! The priest must have told them what I had said, and their answer was wordless — and comical.

It's so interesting the way they have this "free" walk. You have a sense that, as D.T. Suzuki put it, "a Zen monk is a concentration of energy which is available immediately for anything." In one Zen master's writings, this is likened to water in a vessel. If you make a hole in the vessel, the water immediately comes out. It doesn't stop to think about it.

When you clap your hands, the sound is the clapping of the hands. It comes out at once. It doesn't stop to think. When you strike a stone with steel, the sparks fly immediately!

In the same way, as you can see so clearly in the walk of those who practice Zen, there is always availability, always readiness to act. Therefore they live a life which is empty and spacious — in the sense of being "unblocked." To get rid of blocks is to have space in one's life, the same space we've been talking about all along.

The *heart* doctrine of Buddhism, and the final feeling about the universe at the end of the line, when you *really* get down to it, is called in Japanese *ji-ji-muge.* Or in Chinese, *cher cher mu-gai.* Between all things and events in the universe — *muge* — there is no block. In other words, every thing, every event in the universe that ever happens, *implies all the others.*

And the connection between them is:

space.

Which is no block.

If you can see that space is an effective reality, then you can understand the life and death relationship, because you don't need any more information about this relationship than you already have.

When we watch sparrows, this year's sparrows seem to be the same as last year's sparrows coming back again, because we don't pay much attention to the unique individuality of each particular sparrow.

This is in a way like the story of the fisherman who was using worms for bait. Someone came up to him while he was fishing and said, "It's a terribly cruel thing. How can you put those poor little worms on hooks?" And he replied, "Oh, they are used to it."

We look at our own lives from a perspective in which we are enormously preoccupied with the uniqueness of each life. Somebody else at another level of magnification might see human lives as a vast continuity of comings and goings, and they would be just as right from their vantage point as we are from ours — for after all, all these human beings are just different ways of repeating the same event. Whether you call someone Jane or Joan, or John or Peter, it is always the same person coming back with slight variations — there always have to be slight variations because no two things are quite the same. As is said in Pali, the language of the Buddhist texts, "Each incarnation is not the same, yet not another."

Think about what happens when you die. What will it be like to go to sleep and never wake up? You can't even think about what it would be like because you have nothing to compare it to. It isn't like being shut in the dark forever or buried alive. It is like everything you remember before you were born — after all, what happened once can always happen again.

You know very well that after you die, and after everyone else that you have ever known has died, babies of all kinds — human, animal, and vegetable — will be born. And each one of them will feel that it is "I" in the same way as you do, and each will experience itself to be the center of the universe, exactly as you do. And in this sense, then, each one of them is you, for this situation can only be experienced one at a time.

So you will die, and then someone else will be born, but it will feel exactly as you do now. It will be, in other words, "I" — and there is only one "I," although it is infinitely varied. So you don't have to worry; you are not going to sit and wait out eternity in a dark room.

To put this another way, allow me to make two propositions. After I die I will be reborn as another baby, but I will have no memory of my past life. That is proposition number one. Proposition two is simply that after I die another baby will be born. I maintain that these propositions really are the same thing, because if there is no memory of having lived before then effectively that baby *is* someone else. But after a while you have accumulated so many experiences and collected so many memories that they are lined up like a shelf of mystery stories that you have already read, and it comes time to get rid of them.

You want a surprise, a new situation. You do not want to know what the outcome will be. One of the rules of the game of chess is that if you know the outcome of a game for certain, you cancel it and begin a new one in which the outcome is not certain. This is also part of nature, and so we have to have forgetfulness as well as a memory, just as we have to have a capacity to retain food — the stomach and so on — but also a capacity to reject it. We have to have a hole at each end, and so it is with memory.

By being able to lose yourself utterly — everything you have clung to, everything you have built up, all of your accomplishments and your pride — the world may begin anew, and see itself again through your eyes.

PART IV

ZEN MIND

ZEN MIND

If we say that Zen is a certain kind of understanding of the world, or a certain kind of awareness
of the world, we must ask, what kind of awareness is
it? It is very often said that Zen lies beyond the intellect and beyond logic, and that this kind of understanding is not accessible to reasoning or any other
intellectual processes.

What exactly does this mean? From some points
of view, this way of putting it is misleading, because
when we say "intellectualizing" and the Japanese
say "intellectualizing," we don't necessarily mean

the same thing. When in India they say, "The knowledge of Vedanta is not to be obtained from books," this statement has a very specific meaning. It means the books are only lecture notes, and they have to be explained by a teacher.

In the *Yoga Sutra* of Patanjali, the first verse says, "Now yoga is explained." Period. Then the second verse follows. The teachers using these texts know this is just to remind them what to say, in the same way that musical notation for the East Indians is not something you read while you play, it is just to remind you of the basic form of the melody.

The word "now" indicates that something had to go before this; there had to be a preparation before you got to this point in your study of yoga. The word "now" gives the teachers a clue for their pitch.

In the same way, the *Upanishads* in their compact style are simply the notes to accompany the teaching. This is especially true of the *Brahma Sutras*; if you come across Radhakrishna's translation of the *Brahma Sutras* you will find these funny little laconic verses from the sutra, and then pages upon pages of Radhakrishna's commentary. That's one reason why it is said that you can't get it from books.

Another reason is that books by their very nature are intellectual, and the understanding of Zen is intuitive.

What is the difference between intellectual understanding and intuitive understanding? When you talk about these deep matters, people often say, "I understand what you're saying intellectually, but I don't really *feel* it." And I often say, "Well, I don't think you understand it intellectually, because the intellect and the feelings aren't really two different compartments of the mind."

Carl Jung has a schema of the mind as having four functions — intellect, feeling, intuition, and sensation — but these are only colors in a spectrum, as it were. The spectrum of light is continuous, and red is not in a different compartment from blue. Light is all one spectrum, with many colors.

In the same way, we have one mind, and it has various different ways of functioning.

A psychologist was ribbing me a while ago, kidding that I was only proficient in words. "You put on a great talk, but you don't understand it other-wise," he said.

"Don't you put down words like that!" I said, "Words are noises in the air; they are patterns of thought, patterns of intellect, like a fern. Do you put down a fern because it has a complicated pattern?"

"No," he said. "But the fern is real — it's a living, natural thing."

And I said, "So are words! I'll make patterns in the air with words, and make all sorts of concepts and string them together, and they're going to be great! So don't put it down — it's a form of life like any other form of life."

Zen indeed has an intellectual aspect. This aspect is known in Japanese as *kegon*, and in Chinese, *hua-yen*. Hua means the flower, so this is the school of the flower garland.

In Sanskrit, it is what is called *ganda-vyuha*, the most sophisticated form of Mahayana philosophy. When we were talking earlier about *ji-ji-muge*, the mutual interpenetration of all things and events, this is the philosophy that evolved in this school.

The study of yoga has an intellectual aspect, as well. There are various forms of yoga: *bhakti yoga*, which is devotional, emotional, related to feelings; *karma yoga*, which is practical and active; *hatha yoga*, which is physical; and *jnana yoga*, which is intellectual.

But so many people have great difficulty in seeing the bridge between intellectual understanding and intuitive understanding. They know the words, but don't get any real "sense" of the meaning in a way that their sense-experience has changed. When we say "an intuitive understanding," the word "intuition" is subtle, even vague, but "Zen understanding" is sensuous. It is something that you feel not so much in an emotional way as in a direct way, just like when you feel that something is *hard*. As they say, "It is like tasting water and knowing for yourself that it's *cold*." It is sensation, an actual, *physical* sensation.

But how is the intellect related to physical sensation? Or is it completely unrelated? What difference does it make to your sensation whether you think at dawn that the sun is rising or whether you know that the earth is rotating on its axis and revolving around the sun? Is the sensation of a person who does not know that the earth is revolving on its own axis and going around the sun the same as the sensation of a person who does?

Or let's look at another example. There are certain indigenous people in the world whose number system consists of one, two, three, and many. They do not differentiate after "three." For those people it can never be a "fact" that a table has "four" corners — it has "many" corners. So they wouldn't differentiate between a five-cornered and a six-cornered table because they have no "concept system" to give them the cue.

Take an illustration like this — it is very simple, but all depends on concept:

If you have no concept, that drawing is simply a flat-surface pattern. But if it has been explained to you that it is a cube, then you can imagine and actually *sense* the three-dimensionality in it. Now then, let's go further and ask which surface of the cube is in front? Is it the one with corners "A"? Or the one with corners "B"?

You can see it either way, and so you can make either of them the one in "front." Once you've caught on to the idea, it becomes sensation to you — you can actually "feel" it.

This points to the connection between intellect and physical sensation: Concepts lead to sensations — and therefore, false concepts lead to illusions.

We have seen this principle demonstrated before with all kinds of optical illusions. In those illusions our *concept* influences our *sensation*. A central point in Zen is that we have a concept of our own existence and of the world which is fallacious, and Zen will help us get rid of that concept so that we will have a new sensation. People get worried when they hear this, and say, "Well, are we just going to exchange one hallucination for another?"

Let me respond with a question or two: How do

you know when you know that you know? What is the *test* of "truth" about something that you "feel"?

You may say, "Well, I can feel that I'm Napoleon, or that I'm being persecuted by the government." But this is hallucination — even though one might feel it very strongly.

In our culture, we have a "test" of truth, which is science. We say, "If something can be demonstrated scientifically, then we're inclined to believe that it's not hallucination." All right, let's go along with that. I think this is rather relative, but I will always in any argument grant the premises of the person who wants to argue with me, and take it from there. Let's assume that sciences like biology and physics are ways of discovering the "truth." When we grant that, we find that the hallucination of being a separate ego will not stand up to biological tests!

From the point of view of biology, the individual organism is in the same "behavior system" as the environment, and in fact the organism and the environment constitute a single system of behavior which is neither deterministic nor voluntary. The two are really one activity, and they call it the "field of the organism-environment." Ecology is the study of these kinds of fields.

When I am in academic circles, where people so often think that mystical matters are not at all respectable, I don't talk to them about mystical experience. I talk instead about "ecological awareness." It's just a matter of observing current etiquette and nomenclature, because these are two ways of describing the same reality. From a biological point of view it is perfectly clear that every individual instance of life is a function of the whole universe. This becomes even clearer in quantum theory.

Then you might ask this question: "Why do you scientists — biologists and physicists — who understand this to be so still go on behaving as if you were separate egos?" And they would answer that, in spite of the evidence to the contrary, they still *feel* that way. Their theory is only still at the point of being theory, in that it hasn't convinced them so far as they themselves are concerned. They are still under the social hypnosis that we were all conditioned to in childhood that made us feel as if we are separate egos.

So Zen is a process of "de-hypnotization," if you like. Zen takes away the concepts that are much like optical "tricks," concepts that give us the hallucination of separateness.

Then, when we find out what things are like when the concepts have been taken away, we can say to the biologist, "Isn't this just like you said it was?" And he has to agree. What we arrive at is a state of sensation or feeling that is far more in accord with the findings of science than the ordinary sensation we have of being separate individuals.

So the way in which Zen is non-intellectual is not so much that it regards intellection as something always false and misleading; instead, Zen *begins* by taking away our concepts, and by showing us how to see what it is like to view the world without concepts. Once we have discovered this new view of the world, we can re-fabricate new concepts to try and explain *now* how it is that we see.

For this reason, many Zen masters are also great intellectuals. In the history of Zen there have been scholars of all kinds, and physicists in modern times. Zen does not rule out the life of the intellect. It only says, "Do not be hoaxed by concepts."

Is Zen illogical? Illogical is not the right word, because what often appear in Zen to be paradoxes are statements that make perfect sense in another system of logic than that to which we're accustomed. We in the West are accustomed to a kind of logical thinking that is based on exclusiveness — "either-or." Chinese logic, on the other hand, is based on "both-and."

To us it is either "black" or "white," it either "is" or it "is not," it is either "so" or it is "not so." This kind of logic is fundamental to our thinking, and so we emphasize the mutually exclusive character of logical categories: "Is you is or is you ain't?" Is it in the box or outside the box?

In so many of our tests we are asked "true" or "false," "yes" or "no," and we're given *only* those choices. It's amusing to think that when we toss a coin to decide whether we will do it or we won't, we have only a two-sided coin. The Chinese are able to toss a sixty-four-sided coin by using the *Book of Changes* in the same situations where we would toss a coin. It's a rather nice idea, when you think about it, and even though the *Book of Changes* is based on yin and yang, black or white, you can get everything out of black and white if you provide for all of the permutations that are possible — just as you can get all numbers out of zero and one in the binary system. But whereas we think something is either/or — either black or white — both Indian and Chinese logic recognize that black and white are inseparable, that in fact they *need* each other, and so it isn't a matter of making a choice between them.

"To be or not to be" is *not* the question — because you can't have one without the other! Not-being implies being; just as being implies not-being.

The existentialist in the West — who still trembles at the choice between being and not-being and therefore says that anxiety is ontological — hasn't grasped this point yet. When the existentialist who trembles with anxiety before this choice realizes suddenly one day that not-being implies being, the trembling of anxiety turns into the shaking of laughter.

Nothing has changed except one's perception. And in the same way, you may have the same view of the world — just what you're looking at now, seeing everything that you see now — but it can have a completely different feeling, and a completely different meaning to it. Because in one's ordinary sensation of the world the *differentiations* — the solids — are stressed, and the space is ignored.

But when you practice Zen meditation, you have a kind of a "conceptual alteration," and then suddenly you notice the physical world — everything you're seeing now — in a completely different way. You see that it all goes together; it's all-of-a-piece. You see that every inside implies its outside, and every outside implies its inside.

You may think now, in the ordinary way we're conditioned to think, that "I — me, myself — am *only* on the inside of my skin." But when you experience this perceptive "flip," you discover your outside is as much *you* as your inside. You can't have an inside without an outside, so if the inside is yours, then the outside is yours!

Finally you have to acknowledge that the world *outside* your skin is as much yours as the world inside the skin. And even though everybody's outside appears different to us, in reality everybody's outside is all the same! Do you see?

It is in this way that we're one.

Your soul isn't in your body; your body is in your soul!

That's why the ancients were partly correct with their astrology. When they drew a "map" of a person's soul, they drew a crude map of the universe as it was at the moment of the person's birth, seen from that place and time. That map, that horoscope, is considered to be a "picture" of that person's mind — because your mind is not in your head, your head is in your mind. And your mind is the total system of cosmic interrelationships as they are focused at the point that you call "here and now."

The question is then: Can this become clear to us? Can it become clear in the way a *sensation* is clear, as when we taste water and know for ourselves that it is cold? The experience of this requires some meditation, and it also depends on an intellectual process.

We get *into* trouble through an intellectual process and we're going to get *out of* trouble through an intellectual process. From an intellectual standpoint, the process by which we get into trouble could be called "additive," whereas the process by which we get out of trouble is "subtractive." In the words of Lao-tzu, "The scholar gains every day; the man of Tao loses every day."

The scholar acquires ideas, and in Zen the intellectual operation is to get rid of ideas — to see that *all* ideas are projections that we make upon the cosmic Rorschach blot.

The world is a Rorschach blot, full of movement and wiggles. Only when we see straight lines and grid-iron patterns do we know *people* have been around. People are always trying to straighten things out, and so we create straight lines!

Look at how the stars are sprayed across the heavens. In order to "make sense" of the stars, we can get stellar maps and see straight lines joining the stars in various patterns to make up constellations. But all those joining lines are of course projections by which we try to make sense of the stars.

In the same way we make projections upon the surface of nature for the purpose of discussing it with each other — and, inevitably, some person with a strong will and a powerful and compelling personality describes the world in one way, and everybody else agrees with him. That's the way it is. And it's passed down through the generations.

So now, let's go back to seeing that the world is a primordial Rorschach blot. Wiggles of the world unite; you have nothing to lose but your names!

Once you see the movement and the wiggles to be what they are, once you realize that we have created the world from our own projections, you see then that the difference between your *inside* (your ego, your self) and the *outside* (the subject-perceiver and the object-perceived) is artificial.

You can confirm this realization through neurology, because neurologists will tell you that the so-called "external world" that you see is experienced by you only as a state of your own nervous system. What you see out in front of you is an experience in the nerve ganglia in the back of your head, and you have no other awareness of an external world *except in terms of your own body.*

You can infer that your body is, in turn, something "in" the external world, but you only know it by union with it. You are in the external world, and scientist and mystic alike will tell you that you are an inseparable part of it.

Yet "part" isn't even the right word, because the world doesn't have "parts" like an automobile engine — it isn't bolted or screwed together. The world is like a body: When your body was born, it grew not by the addition of "bits," but by an organic process in which the whole thing constellated itself at once. It grew larger and larger, growing from the inside to the outside.

It did it in a field called the *womb.* And the womb could only do it in a field called a *female body.* And a female body could only do it in a field called *human society,* in a field called *the biosphere of the planet Earth.* If you take the body out of its field, it cannot grow.

Blood in a test tube cannot do what blood in the veins does, because all of the body's conditions have to be replicated, and that's impossible in a test tube, because it's a different environment.

Just as words change their meaning in accordance with the context of the sentence, so organisms change their nature in accordance with the context of their environment. Even from this strictly scientific point of view, our body-mind — contrary to what we usually feel — is not something separated from other minds and from the external world. *It is all one process.* If we don't feel that to be so, it is because we have been indoctrinated with concepts that contradict the facts. The concept of what we might call the "Christian ego" simply does not fit in with the facts of life; it has become a social institution that is obsolete.

When we say "social institution," people usually think of things like hospitals, parliaments, police forces, fire departments, and so forth. But marriage is a social institution, the family is a social institution, the clock and the calendar are social institutions, latitude and longitude are social institutions. And *the ego* is a social institution; it is, in other words, a "convention" (from the Latin *convenire*, "to come together"); it is a consensus, an agreement. With it we are agreeing to a set of rules for the purpose of playing a game.

What happens, however, is that we are apt to confuse the rules of our social game with the laws of nature — with the way things are. Even the "laws of nature" are social conventions. Nature does not obey a lawgiver who says, first of all, this is the way things shall be, and then all beetles, all butterflies, all rocks, and so on follow it. The laws of nature are *our* way of describing what we believe to be "regular behavior" in nature.

But what is regular? Interestingly, *regulus* in Latin means a "rule." And what is a rule? It is a ruler — it is marked-out in inches, it is straight, and you measure things with it. But you don't find rulers growing on trees! Nature is all of a piece, and everything in it goes with everything else in it, in an eternal dance. But we chop it so that we can discuss it and even try to rule it.

Laws of nature are therefore tools, like axes,

hammers, and saws; they are instruments we use to control what is going on. To keep in touch, then, with what is really going on in the present, always preserve this careful distinction between the game rules of the human game, and the behavior of the world in itself. It is true that the behavior of the world in itself includes the human games, and it's all a part of nature. But don't try to make the tail wag the dog.

The whole point of Zen is to suspend the rules we have superimposed on things and to see the world as it is — as all of a piece. This has to be done in a special setting of some kind, because you can't just gaily walk out into the street and suspend the rules. And if you do, you'll create traffic confusion of every conceivable kind!

But we can set up a certain environment in which we have an agreement to suspend the rules — that is to say to meditate, to stop thinking for a while, to stop making formulations.

This means, essentially, to *stop talking to yourself.* That is the meaning of the word in Japanese — *munen*

— that is ordinarily translated as "no thought." To meditate is to stop talking to yourself!

We say, "Talking to yourself is the first sign of madness," but we don't follow our own advice. We're talking to ourselves most of the time — and if you talk all the time you've got nothing else to talk about but your own talking! You never listen to what anybody else has to say, without a running commentary of your own talking. And if all you ever listen to is talking — be it your own or other people's — you have nothing to talk about but talk.

You have to *stop talking* in order to have something to talk about!

In the same way, you have to *stop thinking* in order to have something to think about, because otherwise all you're thinking about is thoughts — and that's *scholarship*, as we practice it in the universities today, where we study and write and talk about books about books about books!

In order to be able to symbolize, to think effectively, one has to suspend thought occasionally and be in a state of what I will call "pure sensation." Drink water, and know for yourself that it's cold. Sit, just to sit.

> *Sitting quietly doing nothing.*
> *Spring comes and the grass grows by itself.*

You can take that literally or you can take it symbolically. But that is the meaning of *munen*.

Sometimes the word used is *mushin* — no mind. *Mushin* means being open to the way that the world is experienced sensuously, without the distortion of concepts, so as to find the original nature before any thought is made.

It is the way you experienced it when you were first born, before you thought any thoughts about it! It is called your original mind, or the "root mind."

One of the koans that are studied in the Rinzai school of Zen is: "Who are you before your father and mother conceived you?" You could put it this way: "Who are you before your father and mother bamboozled you!" Conceived is used in the sense of "thought about" you, or taught you to conceive.

What is your original mind? Before all this started, *where were you really?*

To go back to that, you have to take a fresh look at the world. You have to come to it unprejudiced, with your mind wiped *clean*, like a mirror, of all conceptions about life and what it is.

Even now, of course, I am giving you conceptions about the unity of the world and about the process of meditation. And those who understand these words still have difficulty if they've *only* got the conception. It may alter their feeling to some extent, and their sensation, but not nearly as vividly as their sensation will be altered if they look at the world *without any conception at all.*

"Well," you might say, "how can we stop? We think perpetually — we are always talking to ourselves. It's a nervous habit!"

To stop thinking, there are certain technical aids:

Concentrate on breathing, and think of nothing but your breathing — in and out, in and out…. One, two, three, four, five…. One, two, three, four, five.

Or look at a point of light and think of nothing else but the point of light — just concentrate, concentrate, on that light.

Both of these help you to eliminate all concepts from the mind except that which you are concentrating on. The next thing is to get rid of the point you're concentrating on.

Most people think that means a "blank mind," but it doesn't. You concentrate on something in order to cause the thought process, the verbalizing, to stop. Then when you take away the point of concentration, you are simply perceiving the world *as it is*, without verbalizing.

The trick of concentration stops our verbalizing. Concentration is only preliminary. It leads us deeper, beyond concentration, until we reach the state of *samadhi*. This is *dhyana*, in Sanskrit — which came to be called *c'han* in China and *zen* in Japan. It is not concentration in the ordinary sense, like staring at a point or thinking of one thing only. It comes after concentration has stopped, after the point on which you have concentrated has fallen away, after your body and mind have fallen away, and you're open to the world with your naked senses.

See that.

That is the foundation experience.

After you see that, and on the *basis* of seeing that, you can, of course, go back to concepts and construct this idea of the world, that idea, and the other idea.

This is why Zen does not really involve any beliefs in any theory or doctrine. In this sense, it is *not* religion — if by religion you mean something that involves a system of beliefs. It is purely experimental and empirical in its approach, and it allows us to *get rid of belief* — to get rid of all dependence upon words and ideas.

This is not because words and ideas are "evil," nor because they are *necessarily* confusing; it is just because we do happen to be confused by them at this stage in our evolution.

That is really the essential nature of the whole meditation process: the suspension of talking to yourself, either in words or in any other conceptual image.

It is of interest that words are a form of notation — words are the notation of *life*. Just as musical notation is a way of writing down music so as to remember it, words are essential vehicles of memory: we repeat them, we write them down, and we remember. That gives us a wonderful sense of control, but to the extent that we are tied to our notations, we pay a price for it.

In music, notation limits our ability to conceive of variations and other musical forms. The Hindu, however, is not tied to notes in music, and therefore values a kind of music in which a musical instrument — be it a drum, flute, or sitar — is immediately responsive to every subtle motion of the human organism. They therefore play things —

odd quarter-tones and strange rhythms — which are impossible to reproduce with our notation.

The Hindu rejoices in the extreme subtlety of a flute, so responsive to human breath, an organic phenomenon. When they listen to our music, it all sounds very structured and rigid to them, like a military march, because of the regular beat and the fixed harmonic intervals.

In the same way, when you get free from certain fixed concepts of the way the world is, you find it is far more subtle, and far more miraculous, than you thought it was. You find that human relationships and situations are amazingly subtle. And you gain a facility for understanding them, not through con-ceptualizing, but through asking your brain how it would deal with them.

Your brain is an organ like your heart, and it can deal with situations without having to think about them! The brain is not only an organ of thought — only one of its functions is thinking. The brain does a lot of things other than thinking, and enables your body and mind to perceive and act in new, unique, and wonderful ways.

You have a fantastic computer in your skull — and what we call "thinking" is only fifteen percent or less of the brain's activity. The brain is very active in controlling all our organic processes — our gland functions, our digestion, our circulation, and everything else. The brain is in control of the entire autonomic nervous system. Through the practice of Zen, you can learn to use your nervous system in a much more wonderful way than you would ever have thought it could be used!

By practicing Zen, you find you can let your nervous system answer questions and pass through problems without any interference from your conscious thinking process. We cannot solve the puzzle of the Zen koans or of the situations we encounter in life through our conscious thinking process — but the brain will! And the practice of Zen shows us how.

About the Author

Alan Watts was born in England in 1915. Beginning at age sixteen, when he wrote essays for the journal of the Buddhist Lodge in London, he developed a reputation over the next forty years as a foremost interpreter of Eastern philosophies for the West, eventually developing an audience of millions who were enriched through his books, tape recordings, radio and television appearances, and public lectures. He became widely recognized for his Zen writings and for *The Book: On the Taboo Against Knowing Who You Are.*

In all, Watts wrote more than twenty-five

books and recorded hundreds of lectures and seminars, all building toward a personal philosophy he shared with honesty and joy with his readers and listeners throughout the world. His overall works have presented a model of individuality and self-expression that can be matched by few philosophers.

Watts came to the United States in 1938, and earned a Master's Degree in Theology from Seabury-Western Theological Seminary. He was Episcopal Chaplain at Northwestern University during World War II, and held fellowships from Harvard University and the Bollingen Foundation. He became professor and dean of the American Academy of Asian Studies in San Francisco and lectured and traveled widely.

He died in 1973 at his home in northern California, survived by his second wife and seven children. A complete list of his books and tapes may be found at www.alanwatts.com.

The book you have just read was created
from the Alan Watts Electronic University
audio tape archive, a vast library of recordings
of his public lectures and seminars.
The archive is the source of Alan Watts'
audio collections, new publications,
and ongoing public radio programs.

For information about ordering
Alan Watts audio collections,
go to www.alanwatts.com
on the Internet, or write or call:

Electronic University
Post Office Box 2309
San Anselmo, CA 94979

Phone: (800) 969-2887
Catalog request: Ext. 2
Ordering: Ext. 3
E-mail: watts@alanwatts.com